# Looking at . . . Gallimimus

## A Dinosaur from the CRETACEOUS Period

THE NEW
DINOSAUR
COLLECTION

For a free color catalog describing Gareth Stevens' list of high-quality books, call 1-800-542-2595 (USA) or 1-800-461-9120 (Canada). Gareth Stevens' Fax: (414) 225-0377.

Library of Congress Cataloging-in-Publication Data

Brown, Mike, 1947-
    Looking at-- Gallimimus / written by Mike Brown; illustrated by Tony Gibbons.
        p.   cm. -- (The New dinosaur collection)
    Includes index.
    ISBN 0-8368-1142-9
    1. Gallimimus--Juvenile literature.  [1. Gallimimus.  2. Dinosaurs.]  I. Gibbons, Tony, ill.
II. Title.  III. Series.
QE862.S3B775   1994
567.9'7--dc20                                                    94-16967

This North American edition first published in 1994 by
**Gareth Stevens Publishing**
1555 North RiverCenter Drive, Suite 201
Milwaukee, Wisconsin 53212 USA

Consultant: Dr. David Norman, Director of the Sedgwick Museum of Geology, University of Cambridge, England.

Additional artwork by Clare Herronneau.

Printed in the United States of America

1 2 3 4 5 6 7 8 9 99 98 97 96 95 94

At this time, Gareth Stevens, Inc., does not use 100 percent recycled paper, although the paper used in our books does contain about 30 percent recycled fiber.  This decision was made after a careful study of current recycling procedures revealed their dubious environmental benefits.  We will continue to explore recycling options.

# Looking at . . . Gallimimus

## A Dinosaur from the CRETACEOUS Period

by Mike Brown

Illustrated by Tony Gibbons

THE NEW
DINOSAUR
COLLECTION

Gareth Stevens Publishing
MILWAUKEE

# Contents

# Introducing Gallimimus

Many people think all dinosaurs were huge and slow moving, as well as fierce and deadly. But that is not entirely right, as you are about to find out.

Some dinosaurs were very speedy and not monster-like. **Gallimimus** (GAL-EE-<u>MIME</u>-US), for instance, was fast on its feet and not very tall for a dinosaur. One of the dinosaurs featured in the film *Jurassic Park*, **Gallimimus** was one of the most fascinating creatures of its age.

If **Gallimimus** were alive today, you might almost mistake it for an ostrich. Indeed, the name *Gallimimus* means "fowl mimic." It was given this name because its remains show that it must have looked very much like a bird. But it was not a bird, and it could not fly.

Where and when did this dinosaur live? What did it feed on?

And who were its enemies? Join us as we present **Gallimimus**'s exciting life story.

# Ostrich dinosaur

And, like an ostrich, **Gallimimus** could not fly.

**If** humans had existed at the time of **Gallimimus**, about 70 million years ago in the Late Cretaceous Period, you would have been able to spot this dinosaur right away.

**Gallimimus** looked very much like a large bird of the present-day world – an ostrich, to be exact. But, just as there were no humans anywhere on Earth at that time, there were no ostriches, either.

Like today's ostrich, **Gallimimus** was tall, with a long, *S*-shaped neck and a toothless beak.

**But** there were important differences between the two creatures. **Gallimimus** measured about 13 feet (4 meters) long, making it much bigger than an ostrich.

And **Gallimimus** did not have any feathers.

Now let's take a look at **Gallimimus**'s body in detail. Its arms were short, with three-clawed hands. Its tail was long and broad, narrowing toward the tip. The legs were long and slim.

They were still powerful enough, however, for **Gallimimus** to run very swiftly, whether after prey or away from predators. Scientists think **Gallimimus** may also have used its legs to kick out at enemies when it needed to protect itself from a killer carnivore.

No one knows for certain what color **Gallimimus** was – our artist has had to make a guess. We do know, however, that it would have had thick, tough, and scaly skin. The skin was probably like leather and may have had bumps all over it, forming a pebble pattern, as this illustration shows.

Some of these scales may have been round, while others may have had several sides. They probably did not overlap like fish scales do. It is also likely that **Gallimimus**'s belly area was a paler shade than the rest of its body.

7

# Slender

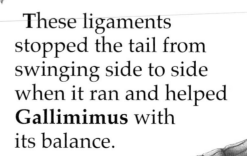

We know about **Gallimimus** from its bones, which have only been found in Mongolia. But there are several skeletons that are well preserved, and from them we can learn much about this ostrichlike dinosaur.

**Gallimimus**'s skeleton shows that it was a champion runner. This dinosaur's legs may seem slim and delicate, but they were extremely strong.

**N**ow examine its feet. They also give us a clear clue that it must have been a great sprinter. The toes are quite long and slender, and its foot bones are even longer. This is very similar to the foot bones of fast-running, ground-living, flightless birds of today, such as emus and rheas.

**Gallimimus** could move its long, graceful neck around quite easily, but its tail was far more rigid. It was held in place by strong ligaments.

These ligaments stopped the tail from swinging side to side when it ran and helped **Gallimimus** with its balance.

# skeleton

**Gallimimus**'s skull was made of thin bone and was lightweight. And wouldn't you agree that its long beak and large eye sockets look like those of a bird?

**I**magine you are a paleontologist. You and your team have just dug up the bones of a dinosaur at a site in Mongolia.

**W**hen you get the skeletal remains back to your laboratory, you will want to identify the dinosaur they belonged to.

**Y**ou all agree that the head seems to be quite small, and there is evidence of there having been a beak. There are no signs of any teeth, however.

**T**he body seems to have been slender, and there are long leg bones. Once the team has put all the neck bones together, you can see how long that was, too. And even though you have not managed to dig up all the tail bones, you can tell that it must have been very long and tapering.

**W**hat a find! You proudly announce another magnificent **Gallimimus** skeleton to the world's press! The reporters ask how it died.

**Y**ou make a guess that some greedy predator must have taken this speedy runner by surprise.

9

# Cretaceous Mongolia

If you could travel back to when **Gallimimus** lived, you would find yourself in the Late Cretaceous Period, in a part of the world now known as Mongolia.

Today, Mongolia is dry and mostly desert. But 70 million years ago, the climate was cooler, and there were many more plants. Among them were conifers, palmlike cycads, and broad-leafed trees. In that era, flowering plants and trees – such as magnolias – were beginning to appear for the first time ever. The many open plains provided fine running country for **Gallimimus**.

**M**any other dinosaurs also lived in Cretaceous Mongolia – **Psittacosaurus** (SI-TAK-OH-SAW-RUS), for instance, a plant-eater with a strange parrot-beak, and the frilled dinosaur **Protoceratops** (PRO-TOE-SER-A-TOPS).

Another plant-eating dinosaur of this time was **Saurolophus** (SAWR-OH-LOAF-US). It had a broad snout and an odd, tube-shaped crest on its head.

**B**ut these plant-eaters did not always have a peaceful time. They had to keep a sharp lookout for hungry meat-eaters, or carnivores. Two such Cretaceous hunters were **Velociraptor** (VEL-O-SI-RAP-TOR), whose name means "speedy robber," and **Oviraptor** (OVE-IH-RAP-TOR), meaning "egg thief."

**A**ll these dinosaurs from Cretaceous Mongolia are shown in this illustration. See if you can identify them.

# Speedy runners

Whoosh! Like lightning, dozens of **Gallimimus** dashed across the plain. They must have been running at speeds of almost 37 miles (60 km) per hour. That's about the speed limit in most towns today.

But why did the **Gallimimus** in the film strip shown here need to run so quickly? Three greedy carnivores, **Saurornithoides** (SAWR-<u>OR</u>-NITH-<u>OID</u>-EEZ), were hungry and on their trail. These were intelligent predators with grasping hands and nasty claws on their second toes.

Even if you ran your fastest, you would never be able to run at that rate. If you have seen the film *Jurassic Park*, you may remember the thundering **Gallimimus** stampede.

As they ran in panic, the **Gallimimus** held out their stiff tails behind them. This helped them balance while running.

Their strides were huge, but would they be able to outrun the terrifying **Saurornithoides**?

The gap between the stampeding **Gallimimus** and the **Saurornithoides** grew larger.

The **Gallimimus** were certainly the faster runners.

One young **Gallimimus** lagged behind and was in danger of being caught by the fearsome predators. Then, suddenly, a giant **Tarbosaurus** (TAR-BO-<u>SAW</u>-RUS) announced its presence with a mighty roar. It was also on the prowl for dinner.

It was a very tiring chase for the smaller **Gallimimus**, however, who found it hard to keep up. Their legs were not so long, and they soon became breathless.

Now it was the **Saurornithoides'** turn to be fearful as **Tarbosaurus** leapt out at them. What a lucky little **Gallimimus**! It was able to make its escape unharmed and return to the herd. Phew!

# Feeding time

**Gallimimus** had no teeth in its beak. It probably ate anything that was small and soft enough to swallow without chewing! So its diet may well have included eggs belonging to other dinosaurs, plants and berries, lizards and insects, and many other small creatures.

**Gallimimus**'s lack of teeth did not allow for good manners. It would snap up berries and insects alike with its horny beak and then swallow them whole with one great gulp. It was not a frightening hunter and not a great meat-eater, so other dinosaurs were not afraid of it.

Some scientists say **Gallimimus** used its claws to scratch at the soil to uncover eggs and roots. It probably also used its claws to hold small prey, although the claws would not have been strong enough to tear tough meat easily.

One thing is certain – **Gallimimus** must have managed to eat enough to give it the strength to run as fast as it did!

# Dinosaurs and birds

One of the most interesting puzzles about dinosaurs is this: are they related to birds? Could the birds of today – from the majestic eagle down to a small canary in a cage – possibly be descendants of the great dinosaurs that once roamed the Earth?

Through careful study of the skeletal remains, Heilmann was able to show how much the body of a dinosaur, like the **Struthiomimus** (STROOTH-EE-OH-MIME-US) below, must have looked like the body of an ostrich, which is a flightless bird.

Dinosaurs, as far as we know, had no feathers. But one man still thought they might be related to birds. He was the Danish scientist Gerhard Heilmann.

Heilmann, however, had one big worry. Birds have collarbones (we also call them wishbones), and dinosaurs, he thought, did not. So how, he wondered, could the two animals be related after all?

In 1926, Heilmann published a book in which he presented the skeletons of both dinosaurs and birds, looking for similarities.

In the end, Heilmann decided that birds may, instead, have evolved from reptiles that lived long before dinosaurs.

Ostrom has found many things in common between these two. And we also now know that some dinosaurs *did* have collarbones.

Some of today's birds also have dinosaurlike toes, and even the structure of their ankles are similar. And birds' feathers may have developed from dinosaur scales.

Today, however, there are some scientists who are also going back to Heilmann's original ideas – but this time with better information.

One man, Professor John Ostrom, has compared skeletons of the earliest known bird – **Archaeopteryx** (AR-KEE-OP-TER-ICKS) – with small, 28-inch (70-centimeter)-long **Compsognathus** (KOMP-SOG-NAY-THUS) from the Late Jurassic Period. You can see them both illustrated here.

So it does seem possible that birds evolved from small dinosaurs of the Jurassic Period.

A canary, like the one in the cage shown here, may have had some most unusual and large-sized ancestors!

17

# Robot dinosaurs

In London's Crystal Palace Park, there are life-size dinosaur models that can be seen among the trees. They have been there since the middle of the last century.

Most of the world's natural history museums also now house very realistic models of dinosaur skeletons. There is a wonderful display at Rapid City in South Dakota, for instance, and also at a prehistoric theme park in Calgary, Canada. In Chorzow, Poland, too, you can visit what is called the Valley of the Dinosaurs. In Taiwan, meanwhile – and in many other parts of the world, including Japan, Germany, the United States, and Great Britain – there are superb robotic exhibits that roar and move, just as scientists believe real dinosaurs would have done.

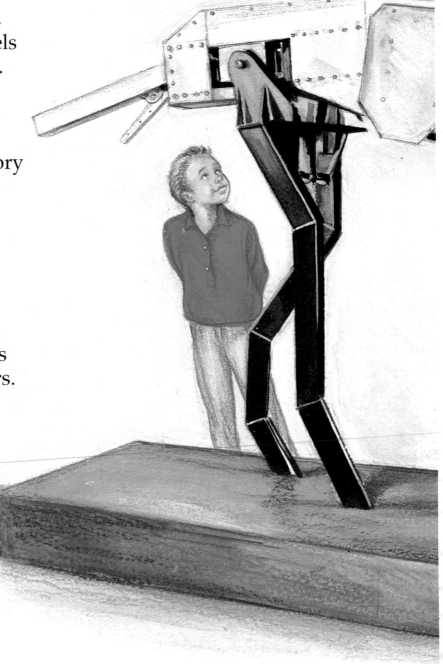

Some of these robotic exhibits have toured the world, too, giving everyone who loves dinosaurs a chance to see and hear them.

Companies who build robotic dinosaurs start by making small models, to scale. Then they construct a skeleton made of steel, to actual size. Here, an engineer is showing the inner workings of a robotic dinosaur to three young visitors to his factory. Next, they will need to make a body of polystyrene and wire. It will hide the machinery that makes the dinosaur move and will be covered by rubber or fiberglass. Which dinosaur do you think it will be?

The model will be painted, of course; and skin texture is made by burning at the surface.

The box of controls is usually in the base of the dinosaur.

Finally, the robotic dinosaur can be switched on. Watch out! It looks so realistic, it might just pounce!

19

# Gallimimus data

There are a number of features that make **Gallimimus** easy to spot when you see a model or a picture of one. Let's examine each feature.

## Long legs

**Gallimimus**'s two back legs were long, thin, and built for great, long strides. If you have ever watched an ostrich run, you will have a good idea of how quickly a **Gallimimus** would have sprinted. If there had been dinosaur Olympics, it would have had a good chance of winning a major track event!

## Slim feet

At the end of its long legs, **Gallimimus** had slim feet. The long foot bones make scientists even more certain it could run at a fantastic rate.

## Toothless beak

This champion runner may often have been able to escape from threatening predators with success. And its great speed no doubt helped it catch lots of small prey, such as insects and lizards. But once it caught a victim, **Gallimimus** could not bite into it, like most other dinosaurs. Because it had no teeth, it had to snap things up in its horny beak and gobble them whole.

## Stiff tail

You have probably noticed that **Gallimimus** had a strong, fairly thick tail that tapered toward the end. **Gallimimus** would hold its tail up when running in order to keep its balance. It is interesting to compare the thickness of its tail with its thin back legs.

## Flexible neck

**Gallimimus** had a long, thin neck, which it held upright when running, just like an ostrich does today. **Gallimimus**'s neck was flexible, too, and could move easily. Being able to look around like this would have helped **Gallimimus** spot a lurking enemy.

## Handy hands

At the end of its fairly long arms – which were a lot shorter than its athletic legs – **Gallimimus** had hands with three clawed fingers. These were useful for grappling with small prey.

## Large eyes

For the size of its head, **Gallimimus** had rather large eyes. This means that it probably had good eyesight and would have been alert for the approach of a predatory carnivore that wanted a meal of **Gallimimus** meat.

# Gallimimus and relatives

**Gallimimus** (**1**) belonged to a group of dinosaurs known as **Ornithomimosaurs** (OR-<u>NITH</u>-OH-<u>MIME</u>-OH-SAWRS). These all had slender limbs and bodies like ostriches, large brains and big eyes, and no teeth. They were probably all omnivores, which means they ate meat and plants.

**Gallimimus** was the tallest dinosaur of this group.

**Elaphrosaurus** (EE-<u>LAF</u>-ROE-<u>SAW</u>-RUS) (**2**) is thought to have been the first **Ornithomimosaur**. It lived in Late Jurassic times, millions of years before **Gallimimus**. We know what its body looked like from a headless skeleton.

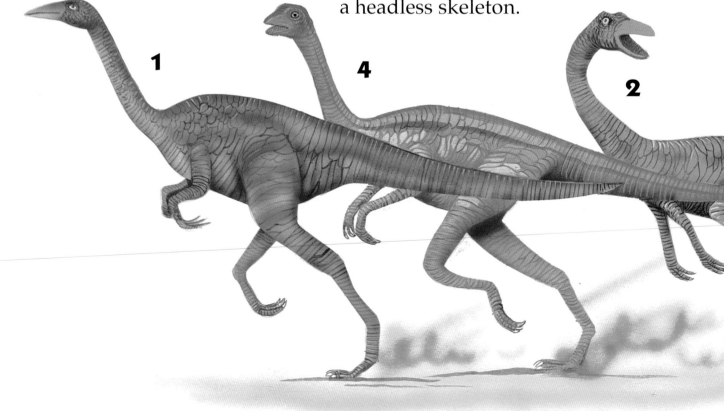

This **Elaphrosaurus** skeleton was found in Tanzania, Africa. However, scientists have only been able to guess at the shape of its head because no skull has yet been found.

**Struthiomimus** (3), whose name means "ostrich mimic," also looked very much like that bird. But, as you can see, like the other **Ornithomimosaurs** shown here, it had no feathers. Like **Gallimimus**, it lived in the Cretaceous Period, in what we now know as North America and Canada. It was about the same size as **Elaphrosaurus**.

Remains of **Ornithomimus** (OR-<u>NITH</u>-OH-<u>MIME</u>-US) (4) were first found in 1889 near Denver, Colorado, and have since also been found in Tibet. This 11-foot (3.5 m)-long dinosaur has a name meaning "bird mimic." It had no teeth but a horny beak, and, once more, a body very much like that of an ostrich. Its arms were thinner than those of its relative, **Struthiomimus**, but overall it was about the same size.

As you can see, about half the body length of these **Ornithomimosaurs** consisted of their tails. And all these relatives were speedy runners.

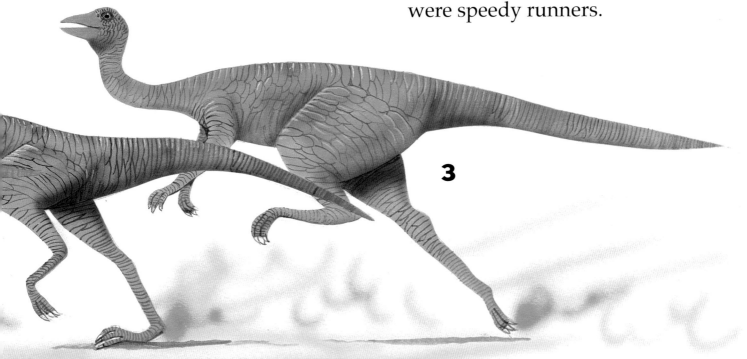

3

# GLOSSARY

**carnivores** — meat-eating animals.

**evolve** — to change shape or develop gradually over a long period of time.

**omnivores** — animals that eat both plants and other animals.

**paleontologists** — scientists who study the remains of plants and animals that lived millions of years ago.

**predators** — animals that capture and kill other animals for food.

**prey** — an animal that is killed for food by another animal.

**remains** — a skeleton, bones, or a dead body.

**reptiles** — cold-blooded animals that have hornlike or scaly skin.

**skeleton** — the bony framework of a body.

**snout** — protruding nose and jaws of an animal.

# INDEX

# The
# WISE MEN Who Found
# CHRISTMAS

### RAYMOND ARROYO

ILLUSTRATED BY DIANE LE FEYER

*To LORENZO, MARIELLA, and ALEXANDER—*
*may you always follow the light just up ahead.*
*—RAA*

*To JULIEN, GAÏA, AND SIRIUS, my shiny stars and my home galaxy.*
*—DLF*

# SOPHIA
## INSTITUTE PRESS

Text Copyright © 2022 by Raymond Arroyo
Images Copyright © 2022 by Diane Le Feyer

Printed in the United States.

Sophia Institute Press
Box 5284, Manchester, NH 03108
1-800-888-9344

www.SophiaInstitute.com
Sophia Institute Press is a registered trademark of Sophia Institute.

Hardcover ISBN: 978-1-64413-620-1

Library of Congress Control Number: 2022941172

2nd Printing

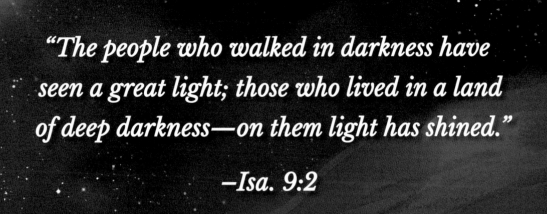

*"The people who walked in darkness have seen a great light; those who lived in a land of deep darkness—on them light has shined."*

*—Isa. 9:2*

There are many tales of the Wise Men
who followed the star to
Bethlehem. But most are untrue.

This is the way I remember it,
and I was there…

In the Arabian kingdom of Nabatea,
atop a temple in the city of Petra,
Magi spotted a star blazing in the sky.

While they all marveled at the sight, only three Wise Men among them debated what it could mean and what they should do about it.

Melchior, the oldest of the Magi, who was very ill,
had heard Jewish prophecies of a Messiah to be
born of a virgin. "Even our own religion foresees
a king who will raise the dead and destroy evil."

Melchior gazed up to the heavens.
"The stars do not lie. He is coming,
and I wish to see him while I can.
We should follow the light."

"If royalty is involved, we should inform our king," said Balthasar, who had spent years at the royal court. "Let him decide our path. Go to the king!"

Then Casper, the youngest, looked to his star charts. "Have you ever seen anything like this? The stars are aligning. We must make haste to discover the truth."

They agreed to share their findings with King Aretas.

The king of Nabatea received his Magi the following night. They showed him how Jupiter and Saturn had come together in the constellation of Aries to create one brilliant star.

"What does it tell us?" Aretas wondered.

"A great king is to be born in Israel," Melchior said.

Now, King Aretas had ties to old, and dangerous, King Herod of Israel. If a new prince were to be born in Israel, surely Herod would know.

"Go to Herod as my representatives," King Aretas ordered.
"Bring this new king offerings from our land."

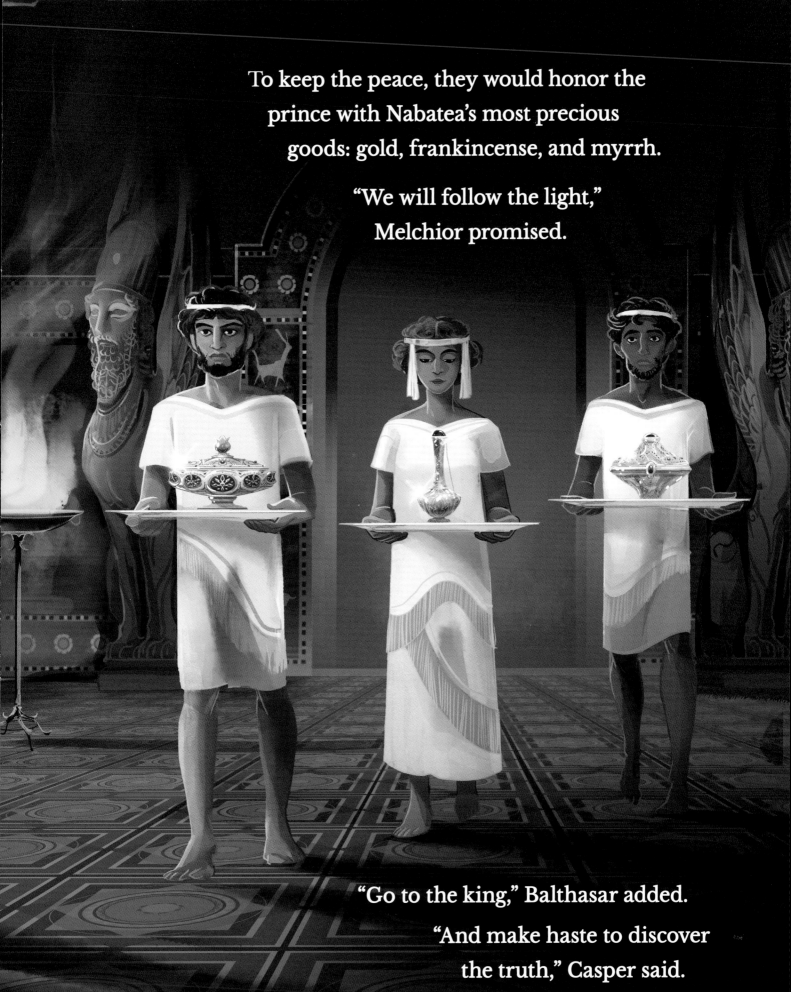

To keep the peace, they would honor the
prince with Nabatea's most precious
goods: gold, frankincense, and myrrh.

"We will follow the light,"
Melchior promised.

"Go to the king," Balthasar added.

"And make haste to discover
the truth," Casper said.

**B**y the time they gathered their caravan
and Melchior mounted his faithful horse,
the star had disappeared from the sky.

Confused and in darkness, the Wise Men galloped
along trade routes they knew well, around the
Dead Sea, past Bethlehem, and on to Jerusalem.

But the ride was long, and old Melchior grew
weary. Though he said nothing, his old bones
plainly ached and his side stung with pain.

After several days, the Wise Men
arrived at the court of Herod the Great.

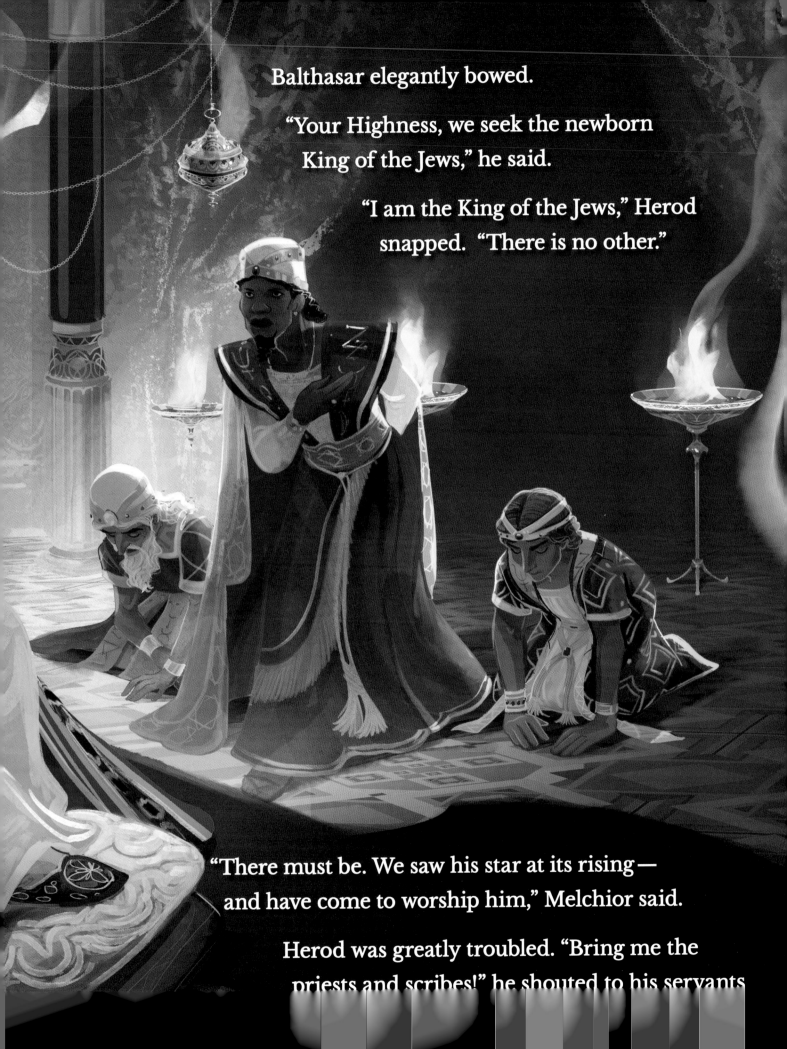

Balthasar elegantly bowed.

"Your Highness, we seek the newborn
King of the Jews," he said.

"I am the King of the Jews," Herod
snapped. "There is no other."

"There must be. We saw his star at its rising—
and have come to worship him," Melchior said.

Herod was greatly troubled. "Bring me the
priests and scribes!" he shouted to his servants

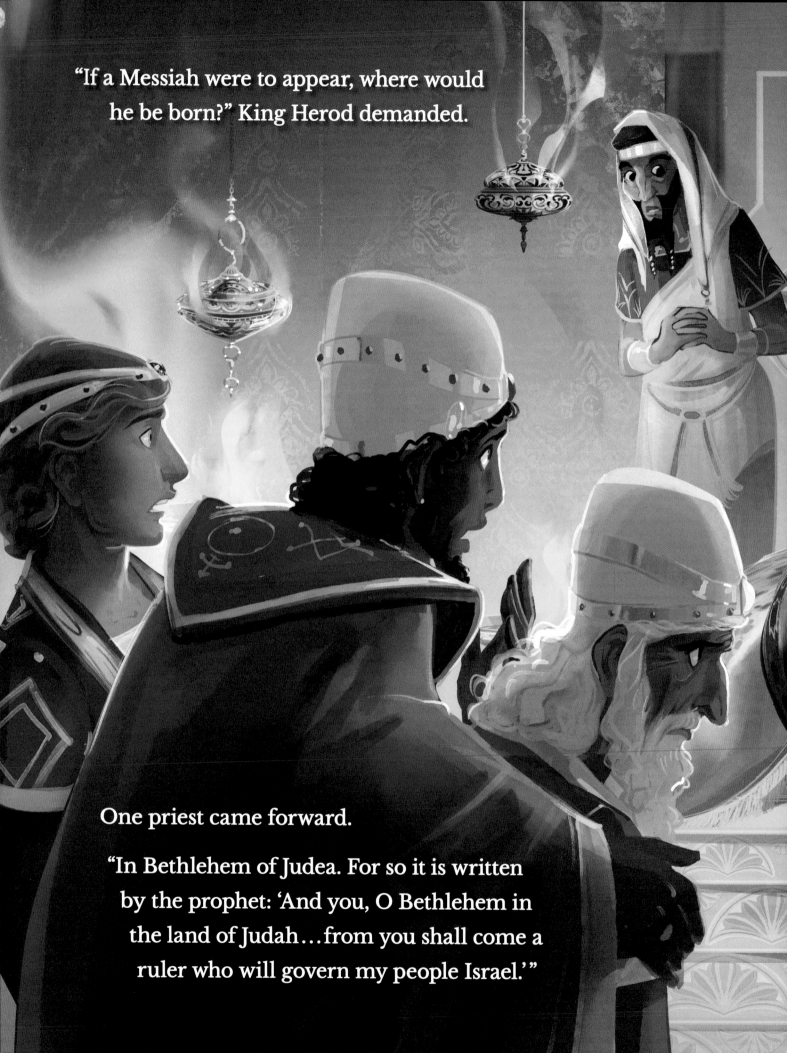

"If a Messiah were to appear, where would he be born?" King Herod demanded.

One priest came forward.

"In Bethlehem of Judea. For so it is written by the prophet: 'And you, O Bethlehem in the land of Judah...from you shall come a ruler who will govern my people Israel.'"

Then the jealous Herod had an idea.
He whispered to the Wise Men:
"Go and search diligently for the child.
And when you have found him send me
word, that I…" A cruel look flashed in his
eyes. "That I too may go and worship him."

The Wise Men nervously bowed
and thanked the old king.

Outside the palace, Casper sighed.
"How will we ever find the child?"

"Perhaps we should go back to
Nabatea," Balthasar suggested.

Melchior felt lost. He hung his head in silence, a hand on his aching side.

That's when Melchior's horse nudged his master's face heavenward.

For in the sky, the star they had
seen in the East rose before them.

The old man yanked at his horse's reins.
"The light. We will follow the light," he said.

"Go to the newborn king?" Balthasar asked.

"Yes," Casper said, dashing ahead of the others. "Make haste to discover the truth!"

Once they reached the little town of Bethlehem, the Wise Men asked the townsfolk where the newborn king might be.

"There is no king here," some said.

"King?" another added. "Herod is our only king."

Then a shepherd told them that one night, as he
tended his sheep, angels appeared in the sky above him.
They told him that a Savior had been born — a tiny
Baby wrapped in swaddling clothes — who the
shepherd later saw with his own eyes.

"Take us to the king!" Balthasar begged.

"I don't know where He is. It was months ago," the
shepherd said. "But He is with us. The Child lives."

Melchior focused on the moving star blazing overhead.

"The light will show us the way to the Child. It will not fail us."

And though members of
the caravan grumbled, the
Wise Men pressed forward.

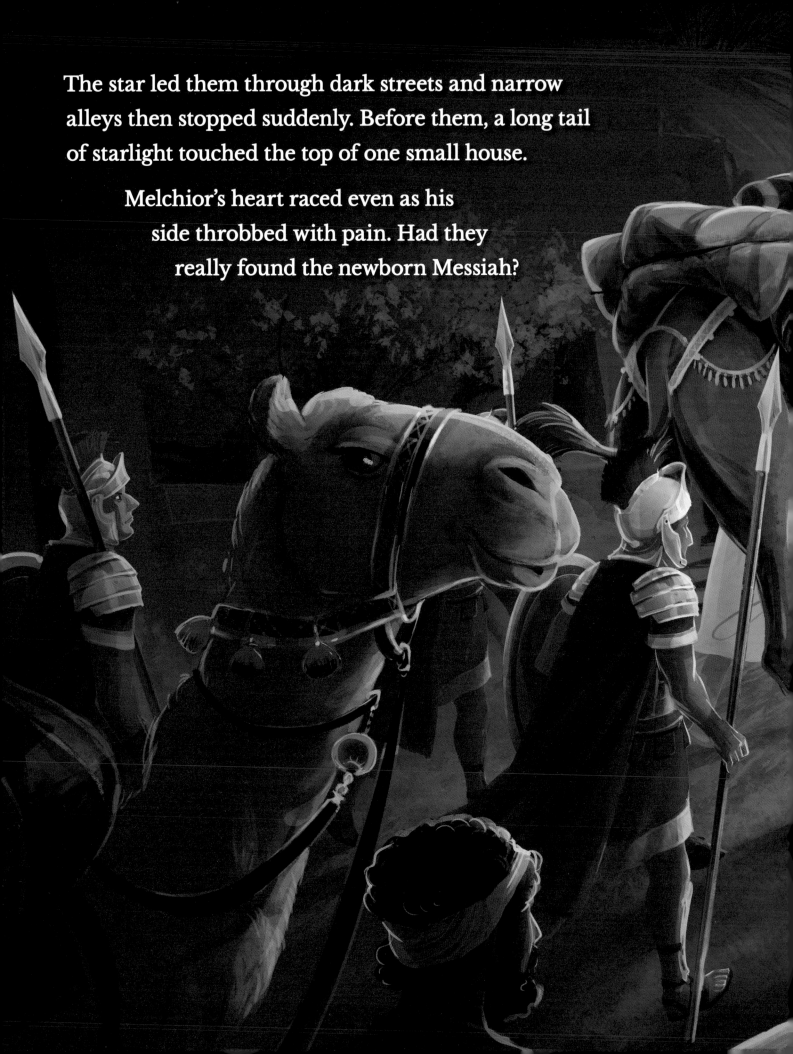

The star led them through dark streets and narrow alleys then stopped suddenly. Before them, a long tail of starlight touched the top of one small house.

Melchior's heart raced even as his side throbbed with pain. Had they really found the newborn Messiah?

Balthasar frowned in bewilderment.
How could this humble home hold a king?

But Casper stomped out an excited
little dance, grabbing the cask of
frankincense from one of the camels.

Then Melchior noticed something odd.

He had assumed that the radiant beam of starlight spilled
down from above. But he now realized that the light actually
shot up to the star from an opening in the roof of the house.

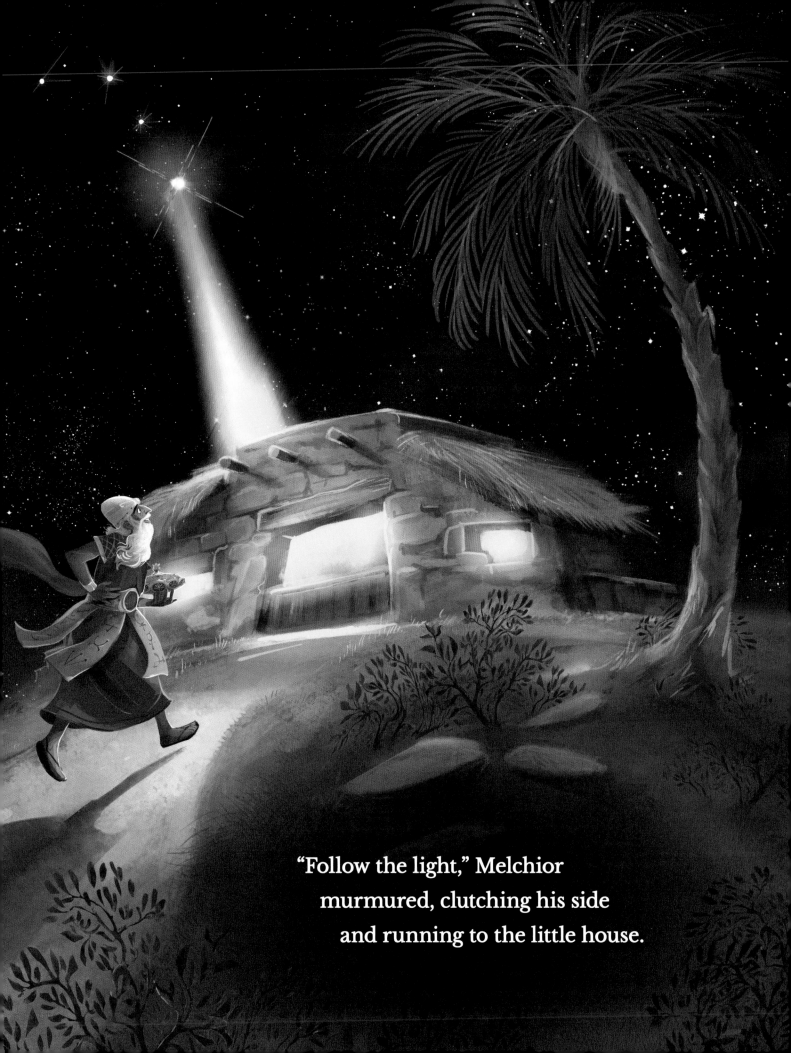

"Follow the light," Melchior
murmured, clutching his side
and running to the little house.

Inside, the Wise Men found the One they sought: a newborn Child in a cradle. Mary, the Child's mother, welcomed them.

"You have come from the East. He has been awaiting your arrival."

For the first time in his long life, Melchior was speechless. The glow of the Child filled him with awe.

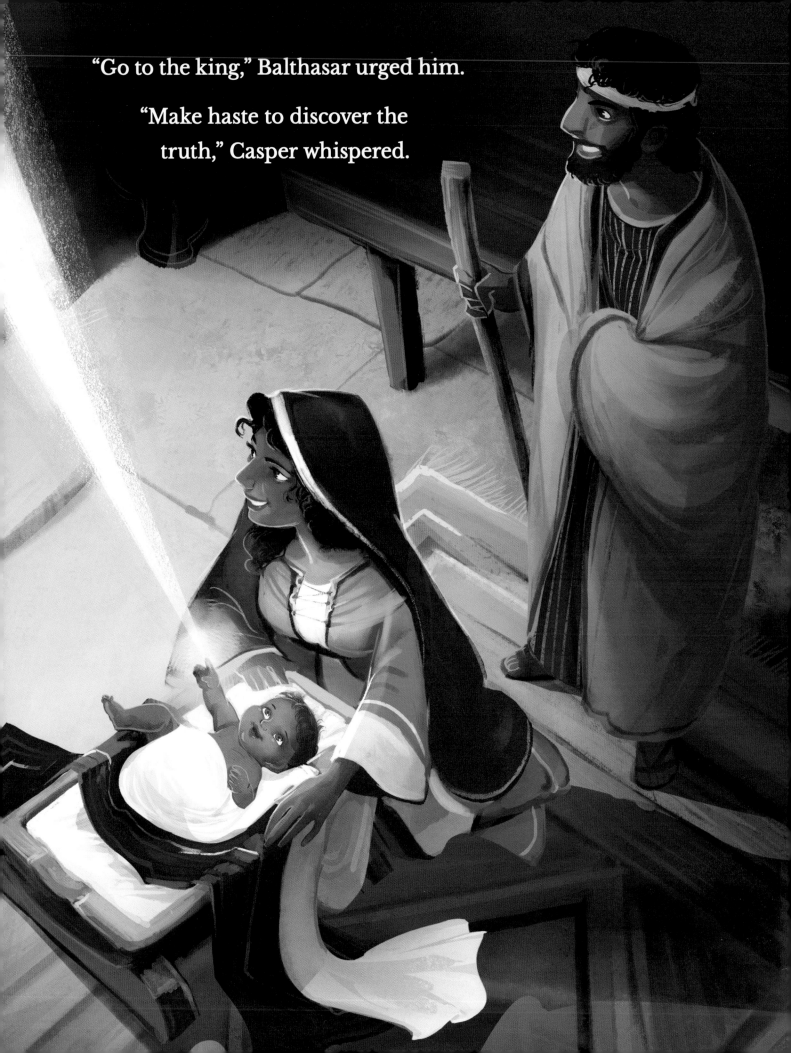

"Go to the king," Balthasar urged him.

"Make haste to discover the truth," Casper whispered.

Each of the Wise Men knelt down
and worshipped the Baby Jesus,
presenting their gifts of
gold, frankincense, and myrrh.

Mary then placed the
Babe in Melchior's arms.

In a hush, the old man told the Child things held deep
in his heart: his desire to see this King whose star he'd
witnessed at its rising, of their long and confusing
journey, and of the illness that had weakened him.

When he returned the Baby to the cradle, Melchior's face shone

"Are you all right?" Caspar asked Melchior as they departed.

Melchior touched his side.

"I have no pain. The Child has healed me."

What wonders we have seen this night," Balthasar marveled.
"Should we go tell King Herod?"

"Not yet," Melchior said. "We will camp here tonight
and then proceed to Jerusalem in the morning."

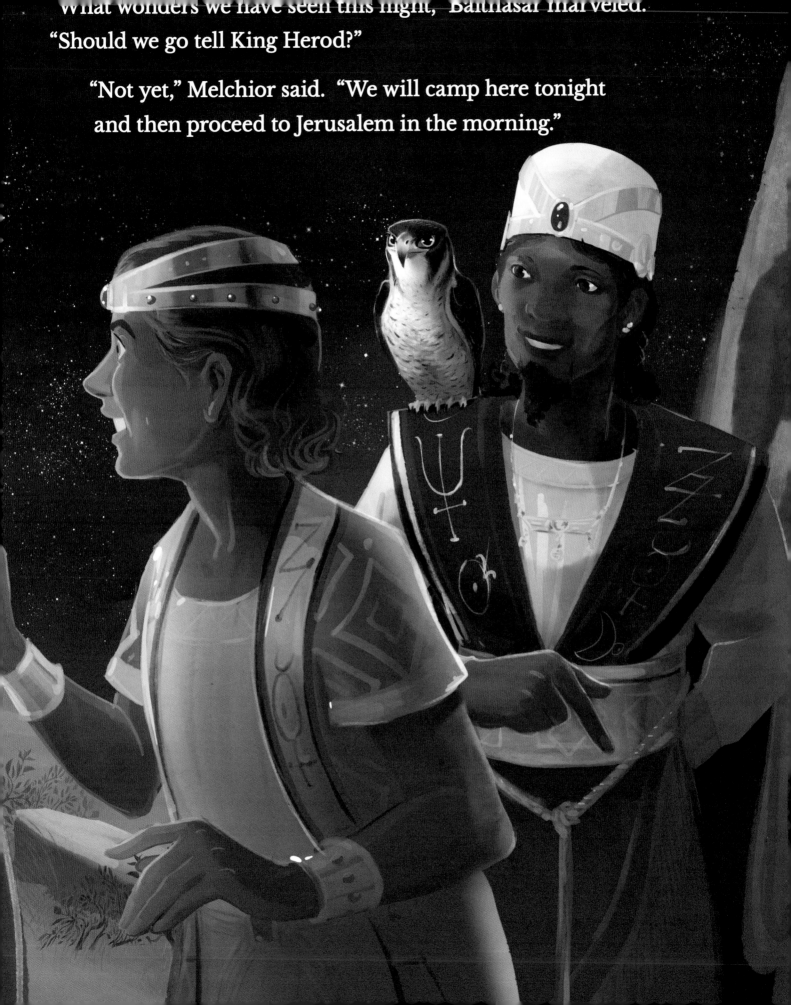

And as they slept,
Melchior, Balthasar, and Casper
dreamed the same dream:

A bright star appeared before them and
transformed into an angel.

"Be not afraid. I have been with you from the
beginning," it announced.  "If you return to
Herod you will place yourselves and the Child
Jesus in great danger. Go home another way."

In the morning, each Wise Man
did as he was told and headed
home on an entirely new path.

For the rest of his days, Melchior
continued to *follow the light*
and spread it to others.

Balthasar no longer cared about the royal
courts of the world. But never stopped
urging those he met to "*go to the King*" — the
smallest he had ever worshipped.

And deep into old age, Casper, with *haste*, passed
*the truth he had discovered* on to any who would listen.

And the Light the Wise Men
found in Bethlehem, centuries ago,
shines still for all who seek it.

I should know…

I saw it myself
and carried the tale.

As you can tell, in this story, the Wise Men are not "three kings" from Asia ("the Orient") or even Persia. Those were pious fictions added to the Magi's story over time. I wrote this version of the tale to rescue the Wise Men from the fictional embellishments and to return them to their historical roots. One traditional aspect I retained were the Wise Men's names—Melchior, Balthasar, and Casper—though those names (which mean "king" in various tongues) don't appear until the fifth century. It was the Venerable Bede, a fifth-century scholar, who noted the ages of the Wise Men, which I imported into my version of their story.

Who were these Magi? They were likely Zoroastrian priests, mathematicians, theologians, stargazers, magicians, interpreters of dreams, and royal consults. Saints and scribes writing in the first and second centuries, including Clement of Rome, describe the Magi as coming from "East of Judea," or northern Arabia. Justin Martyr, writing less than a hundred years after Jesus' Resurrection, tells us: "The Magi came from Arabia and worshipped Him.... These Magi from Arabia came to Bethlehem." The idea that the Magi hailed from Persia—never mind from even farther east—did not appear for hundreds of years later.

I was heavily influenced by the research of Fr. Dwight Longenecker, Dr. Margaret Barker, and John Healey, all of whom offer evidence that the Wise Men may have hailed from Northern Arabia and could well have been Nabatean Magi. Nabatea was not only east of Israel, but it controlled gold mines and the trading routes for frankincense and myrrh. Since Herod controlled the port of Gaza, at the end of the trade routes, it would have been important for the king of Nabatea to maintain good relations with the murderous ruler—and this also explains why he might send a diplomatic mission to offer tribute to any new king of Judea. Nabatea's major city Petra (known to them as Requem) also boasted an eclectic mash-up of cultures, where Arab, Greek, Persian, and Jewish populations shared ideas and beliefs. This would have furnished the Nabatean Magi with an understanding of both the Jewish prophecies as well as the Persian and Greek astral knowledge to interpret the stars.

Just what the star of Bethlehem actually was is a source of endless speculation. Was it a series of astral events? A blazing comet? No one really knows. But the theory I subscribe to is that the Wise Men saw the conjunction of Jupiter and Saturn in the constellation of Aries. Astronomer Michael Molnar believes that these ancient astrologers would have interpreted Jupiter as the star of royalty and would have equated Aries with Judea.

Whatever the facts, these historical clues give us new insight into the determination, grit, and daring of the Wise Men. The lengths to which they went to pursue their beliefs and to track this newborn king are impressive. Herod was also no kindly figure. He even had his own sons killed to protect his power and throne — which sheds new understanding on his determination to remove any new "king of the Jews." In the final analysis, the Wise Men's journey is not some staid, royal procession but a high-stakes adventure filled with setbacks, dangers, and miracles. Perhaps their story holds a lesson for all wise men and women this Christmas:

*Follow the light, go to the King,*
*and make haste to discover the truth.*